Original title:
The Mango's Mystery

Author: Henry Beaumont
ISBN HARDBACK: 978-1-80586-355-7
ISBN PAPERBACK: 978-1-80586-827-9

Chronicles of a Sunset Fruit

In a garden bright and sunny,
There lives a fruit that's sweet and funny.
With a grin that rivals the sun,
It promises a taste that's second to none.

One day it slipped into a pot,
Teasing the chef, oh what a plot!
"I'm juicy, ripe and full of cheer!"
But the chef just sighed, "Not in my sphere!"

Then a squirrel came, with a twitching tail,
He thought it grand, without a fail.
"I'll take the risk for a fruity spree!"
He mumbled aloud, climbing a tree.

With a slip and a slide, he lost his grip,
Landed in a bowl, took a wondrous trip.
The fruit just laughed, what a wild ride,
As the squirrel squeaked, “Let's not abide!”

So if you stroll through a sunny glade,
Look for the fruit who's never afraid.
With secrets tucked in its golden skin,
A slice of joy, where laughter begins.

The Sweetness of the Unknown

In the tree, a treasure hangs,
A yellow globe, where laughter sang.
With every bite, a giggle spills,
As sticky juice drips down in swells.

Eager tongues await the taste,
A fruity prank, oh what a waste!
The pits are tricky, they hide with glee,
In a slippery dance, they fool you and me.

A Serenade of Golden Slices

Oh fruity serenade, how you cheer,
With golden slices that disappear.
A bite of joy, a taste of wit,
Each little chunk a jester's hit.

With dribbles bright on eager chins,
The laughter flows, let fun begins.
Crowned with sweetness, nature's jest,
Who knew a fruit could entertain the best?

Nature’s Juicy Puzzle

In the grove, a riddle sways,
What’s yellow, slippery, in sunshine's rays?
You peel and slice, but still it grins,
A playful tease where the fun begins.

Each chunk a clue in flavors bold,
A jigsaw piece, a story told.
With giggles shared, we roam the feast,
It’s nature's prank on the very least.

The Tropics' Hidden Story

In tropic lands, a tale unfolds,
Of a fruit that giggles and never scolds.
Underneath the leaves, secrets lie,
In every bite, a joyful cry.

Mysteries wrapped in a soft, sweet skin,
Each nibble sparks a silly grin.
From tangy twists to syrupy falls,
The tropics laugh, oh how it calls!

Underneath the Golden Skin

A fruit so bright, it catches eyes,
With juicy treasure, it's no surprise.
But peeling back that sunny shield,
A sticky battle has revealed!

With every bite, sweet drips cascade,
A laugh erupts—what a charade!
My fingers slip, my shirt now stained,
This fruity fun can't be contained!

Labyrinth of Juice and Joy

In the realm of fruity delight,
With giggles echoing day and night.
A pit awaits, oh what a game,
I think I'll win, but who's to blame?

The juices spill, oh what a mess,
My friends all cheer, I must confess!
We race to eat, who'll be the champ?
But the sticky floor? A fruit trap ramp!

The Scented Reverie

A whiff so bold, it calls my name,
Like candy dreams, it's all a game.
I sniff around, and take a chance,
But woe! A bee joins in the dance!

With laughter loud, we make a dash,
As fruit drips down—a yellow splash.
Yet in the chaos, joy we find,
Sweet scent and smiles—so intertwined!

A Fleeting Taste of Paradise

In a sunny patch, we gather round,
With laughter bright, no worries found.
A slice of bliss, I wield my knife,
But can’t escape the drippy strife!

As chunks appear, we take our share,
A fruity feast fills all the air.
And though it ends, this happy quest,
Not just the fruit, but friends are best!

Enchanted Drops of Sunlight

In the orchard, magic swirls,
Sunshine dances, laughter twirls.
A fruit so round, it grins so wide,
Its vibrant hue, a festive ride.

Beneath the leaves, a secret scheme,
Fuzzy squirrels plot, and giggle, it seems.
They seek the treasure, sweet and bold,
With juicy tales waiting to unfold.

A Journey Through Fruity Realms

Take a trip where colors shine,
A road of sweetness, truly divine.
Roll with grapes and dance with pears,
Wobbly melons caught unaware.

In this place, the flavors fight,
Bananas giggle, what a sight!
Ripe delights that conspire,
To tease the taste buds and inspire.

The Palette of an Orchard

In this canvas made of green,
Painted fruits that gleam and preen.
A brush with zest, a swirl of cheer,
Lime and berry, all gathered here.

Each bite a splash, a color burst,
In juicy chaos, we'll bubble and burst.
A fruity art that's sure to please,
Masterpieces made with perfect ease.

Whispered Promises of a Summer Bite

Under sunbeams, sweet whispers play,
Secrets of flavor gently sway.
Crack open joy, let sweetness reign,
Laughing together in summer's domain.

Each juicy morsel a playful tease,
Laughter pops like bubbles in breeze.
So grab a slice, let flavors collide,
In the joyful journey, let laughter ride.

A Dance of Flavor and Fragrance

In a grove where sweetness sways,
Laughter tumbles in bright rays.
Round and round they twist and prance,
Juicy fruits lead a silly dance.

Bouncing bees hum a cheerful tune,
While the breeze tickles, oh so soon.
Colors pop in a fruity show,
Nature's jesters steal the glow.

Fragrant whispers float on air,
Fruits with attitude, they declare.
Each bite's a giggle, zesty flight,
Sour and sweet, a fun delight.

In this carnival of taste,
No droplet goes to waste.
Let's salsa with each juicy bite,
A comedy of flavors, pure delight!

Beneath the Juicy Expanse

Underneath the leafy veil,
A fruity tale begins to sail.
Shadows play in dappled light,
Giggling fruits, oh what a sight.

Plump and silly, they bounce around,
Each one's a clown without a sound.
In this bizarre fruity land,
Laughter grows like grains of sand.

Taste buds giggle, grinning wide,
As tongue-tied tongues take a ride.
Beneath the trees, mischief flows,
With sticky smiles, the fun just grows.

So let’s dive into this spree,
Join the fruity jubilee!
Under the vast and juicy dome,
Adventures wait for us to roam!

Footprints on the Yellow Path

On a path of golden cheer,
Footprints lead, no need to steer.
Each step's a splash of flavor bold,
Stories of fruit, waiting to be told.

With each bite, a giggly shout,
Yummy joy, there’s no doubt!
Step by step, we skip along,
To the rhythm of a fruity song.

Wobbling wonders, cheeky and ripe,
Gathering tales for our next hype.
Each footprint leaves a juicy trace,
In this funny, fruity race!

So follow me, let’s take a chance,
In a world where flavors dance.
Each footfall brings a smile and glee,
What a wacky way to be free!

Echoes of Sun-Kissed Bliss

In the sun’s warm, bright embrace,
Fruity laughter fills the space.
Each juicy orb, a playful tease,
Echoes of joy rustle the leaves.

Silly tales of tangy fun,
Dancing rays, we’re never done.
With sticky fingers and grins so wide,
We’re pirates of flavor, full of pride.

Echoing laughs like chimes of glee,
What treasures wait for you and me?
In this land where fruit flies high,
The sweetest stories never die.

So come along, don’t miss a beat,
Join the chorus of sunshine sweet.
In echoes bright, we’ll find our bliss,
Amidst the fruit, don’t you dare miss!

Sweetness Cloaked in Mystery

In the orchard, a fruit so bright,
Hides a secret, oh what a sight!
Peeling back layers, what will I find?
A flavor that dances, playful and kind.

Under the leaves, whispers abound,
Is it a gem, or a clown on the ground?
With each juicy bite, laughter takes flight,
Who knew such sweetness could cause such delight?

Beneath the skin, a giggling surprise,
It tickles my taste buds and makes them rise.
Each slice reveals a chuckle so bold,
A story unwritten, waiting to unfold.

Unfolding the Enchanted Fruit

A fruit with a smile, so golden and round,
Unfolding its tales without making a sound.
Each nibble a riddle, each taste a jest,
What hides in this morsel? Oh, I must guess!

It wiggles and jives right into my mouth,
Spilling out giggles, going south.
From tree to my belly, it jumps in a flash,
Could it be magic? Or just a sweet splash?

Banana’s been called, ‘I'm the king of the fruit!’
But this one just laughs, ‘Oh, that’s pretty cute!’
With every delicious, sly little bite,
I’m wrangling with joy that feels just right.

Tales from a Sun-Kissed Orchard

In sunlight, they bask, the fruits of delight,
Crafting goofy moments, oh what a sight!
With sticky-fingered smiles, we pluck and we munch,
Each bite, a new giggle, a playful crunch.

Rumors abound of the fruit's disguise,
Whispers of sweetness, and truth in their lies.
Are they jesters of joy, or kings of the sun?
In every sweet morsel, we laugh and we run.

The trees hold secrets under their leaves,
Stories of laughter the bough always weaves.
Juicy and jolly, they dance in the breeze,
In this sun-kissed kingdom, life's a tease.

The Juicy Secrets of Life

What's hidden inside this golden delight?
A giggling mystery, just out of sight.
With every sweet bite, a chuckle is spun,
Revealing the secrets where laughter's begun.

It's soft and it bounces, a trickster at heart,
When shared with a friend, it's pure culinary art!
Taste buds are tickling, oh what a tease,
This juicy escapade brings people to knees.

As I devour the sweetness, I ponder and muse,
What made this fruit gleeful with hints of the blues?
Perhaps in its essence is folly and light,
A jubilant treasure that feels just right.

Treasure Under the Canopy

Beneath the leaves, where shadows play,
A treasure hides in bright array.
The branches giggle, rich and spry,
While squirrels scout and butterflies fly.

One little fruit, round and so sweet,
Smiling down from its leafy seat.
But watch out, folks, it's quite a tease,
It drops with glee, bringing folks to their knees!

Beneath the sun, a laugh we share,
As sticky juice gets caught in hair.
We wrestle with nature, slip and fall,
But oh, dear friends, we love it all!

So join the fun, in this green dome,
Where fruity antics find a home.
The grass is soft, the laughter loud,
In this wild world, we're awfully proud.

Love Letters from the Tree

A love note spills from branches high,
An orange heart that flirts and flies.
It winks and sways, a cheeky grin,
With every gust, it pulls us in.

The letters are strewn like autumn leaves,
Whispers of sweetness nobody believes.
Each sticky hug, a promise sweet,
Entwined in laughter, what a treat!

The birds are chattering, gossiping loud,
Join us now, we'll form a crowd.
Peeling back secrets with every bite,
This fruity love is pure delight!

So take a chance under the trees,
Where love letters float in the breeze.
With every taste, the giggles grow,
In this fruity tale, we steal the show.

Fruitful Enigma

A riddle bursts, with color bright,
Hiding flavors just out of sight.
What’s this orb that swings and sways?
The answer comes in fruity ways!

With laughter dancing in the air,
We poke and prod, with utmost care.
Is it a gem, or sweet delight?
With every taste, we’re filled with fright.

The juice runs fast, wild and free,
A game of hide and seek, oh me!
Each bite reveals a zany plot,
What’s next, we ponder? Still a lot!

So gather ‘round, let’s solve this scene,
With silly grins and jaws unseen.
In this orchard maze, we spin and glide,
Unraveling secrets, oh what fun we ride!

Juicy Secrets Unveiled

In sunlight’s glow, secrets unfold,
A story sweet, both funny and bold.
With each squish and every splat,
We giggle hard, we may fall flat.

The fruit looks round, a playful tease,
It hides its tricks with agile ease.
Catch and splash, a juicy spree,
A sweet surprise, as fun can be!

The laughter bubbles, as sips we share,
All sticky fingers and messy hair.
With every taste, we've formed a crew,
Juicy secrets now come into view!

Join in the fun, let’s play today,
With fruity giggles in sweet ballet.
This orchard’s ours, let’s lift the veil,
And savor the joy in every tale!

Tales from the Mango Tree

Underneath the boughs so wide,
Wiggling ants take a fun ride.
A squirrel steals a slice of sun,
While birds chit-chat just for fun.

A mango dropped, it made a splash,
A puppy slipped, oh what a crash!
Laughter echoed all around,
As everyone fell to the ground.

The tree shook as giggles grew,
With mangoes yellow, green, and blue.
The treasure lies high up, they say,
But birds know how to steal the day!

In the shade, where secrets bloom,
A dance of shadows starts to loom.
Mysteries wrapped in leafy cheer,
The tree knows all, or so we fear!

The Lush Chronicles

In a realm of colors bright,
A farmer swears he saw a flight.
The fruits do giggle, shake, and sway,
There's mischief here, come what may.

Beneath the leaves, a lizard grins,
While mangoes whisper of their sins.
They plot and scheme, a fruity team,
Conspiring for a silly dream.

A round of chuckles fills the air,
As one falls down—who'll get the pair?
Like lead balloons, they land with flair,
Confetti bursting from the air!

In lushness wild, the tales unwind,
Where even worms have fun, you'll find.
So take a seat, laugh and ponder,
At wonders here, we can't help but wander.

Nectar of the Unknown

A sticky finger, a juicy bite,
What’s this fruit? It’s quite a sight!
A taste that sends you round the bend,
A mystery we can't comprehend.

With every splash of yellow gold,
A saga of delight unfolds.
Do mangoes giggle? Oh, who knows!
In juicy whispers, laughter flows.

The droppers dive and munch with glee,
While bees take part in this spree.
In buzzing chorus, they unite,
In nectar dreams, all feels so right.

So join the feast where joy’s the law,
Beneath the bright, sweet, sticky maw!
For in each bite, the fun erupts,
A juicy wonder that corrupts.

Sun-Drenched Whimsy

When sunlight kisses every leaf,
Mangoes giggle, what a relief!
Children chase in playful glee,
While juice drips—who'll catch the spree?

The shadows dance, the laughter sings,
As high above, a birdling swings.
"Catch me if you can!" it teases,
While down below, the joy just pleases.

A fruit so ripe, it rolls away,
A game of tag, they yell and play.
From tree to ground, the chase is on,
In sun-kissed fun, they laugh till dawn.

With every bite, a story's spun,
In sun-drenched mirth, we all are one.
It's just a fruit, yet so much more,
An endless summer to explore!

Navigating the Fruitful Veil

In a grove bright and sunny,
A fruit hangs, plump and funny.
I reach for its golden glow,
But where it goes, I do not know.

It dances like a whiskered cat,
It rolls away, just like that.
A chase ensues, a wild spree,
Who knew a fruit could tease me?

With every twist and every turn,
My thoughts ignite, my taste buds yearn.
But just when it seems I have won,
It pops away, oh what fun!

A surprise awaits, my heart in knots,
This fruit is sly, it has great plots.
In laughter's grip, I find relief,
A riddle wrapped, oh sweet mischief!

Layers of Sugar and Wonder

Beneath its skin, a secret lies,
A treasure wrapped in golden guise.
Each bite, a giggle, smooth delight,
Yet it tricks me, oh what a sight!

With every taste, a tale unfolds,
Whispered laughs in stories told.
One moment sweet, the next a tease,
How can something cause such unease?

I peel it back, excitement swells,
Scented jokes and fruity spells.
A jesting hue, a playful grin,
What game is this, where do I begin?

Oh layers crisp, of joy and play,
This fruit connects us in its way.
In laughter’s court, we share our jest,
Unraveled joy, this fruit's the best!

A Symphony of Succulent Senses

A symphony of skies and zest,
Each note a fruit, a jovial quest.
With melodies that dance and sway,
What treasures wait for me today?

From tangy twirls to sweetened hums,
My taste buds sing as laughter drums.
Each bite a chorus, bold and bright,
This playful feast, oh what delight!

But as I savor, one mischievous bite,
It rolls away—now that's a sight!
A fruit with rhythm, cunning and sly,
I chase it down, oh my, oh my!

In every twist, a giggle stirs,
Each juicy drumbeat, laughter purrs.
This fruity band will steal the show,
In sweet symphony, let's take it slow!

A Taste of Forgotten Dreams

In dreams of flavors long ago,
I chase a fruit, it steals the show.
With hints of laughter on the breeze,
It sways along with such sweet ease.

Memories swirl in golden hues,
Yet this fruit paints a path to choose.
With every crunch, I'm lost in glee,
What mysteries hide inside, oh me!

It tantalizes, I take a bite,
Only to find it's out of sight.
A jest of nature, quick and spry,
This fruity phantom makes me sigh.

Oh taste of dreams I used to know,
You bring some fun, a playful flow.
In laughter's twist, I find my spark,
This fruity chase ignites the dark!

Garden of Hidden Flavors

In a garden bright and vast,
Fruits pop up like jokes so fast.
Lemons smile with sunny glee,
While grapes chat in harmony.

An avocado wears a crown,
Doing pirouettes all around.
Radishes try to steal the show,
But carrots giggle below low.

A peach dresses like a clown,
Sliding down from its tree frown.
Each bite brings a goofy thrill,
Like laughter shared on a hill.

But beware the cherry's plot,
It hides sweet tricks in every lot.
The more you taste, the more you find,
Flavors funny, one of a kind.

Tales of Sugary Shadows

In shadows soft, mangoes scheme,
Hatching visions like a dream.
Kiwis whisper secret charms,
As bananas flaunt their arms.

Peaches plotting juicy pranks,
Laugh at all the fruitless flanks.
A custard apple sings a tune,
Underneath the glowing moon.

Watermelon starts a dance,
While limes just take a silly stance.
Funny tales unfold with ease,
As oranges giggle in the breeze.

So join the fruits, a merry crowd,
Their laughter echoes nice and loud.
With every crunch, a twist awaits,
In sugary shadows, joy celebrates.

Secrets of the Lush Grove

In the lush grove, secrets thrive,
Where fruits come to dance and jive.
Avocados argue who is right,
While coconuts take to flight.

Mangoes hide behind the leaves,
Whispering tales that none believes.
Papaya tricks the roguish bee,
With jokes sweet as honey tea.

Raspberry giggles, polka dots,
While strawberries tell funny plots.
All unite in fruity cheer,
Creating laughter, bright and clear.

Banana slips, a comedic act,
As guava joins in, that's a fact!
In this grove, each twist and turn,
Leaves you chuckling, hearts to burn.

Bounty in the Brightness

In the brightness, fruits collide,
Juggling joy, they take a ride.
Mangoes roll like little clowns,
As blueberries wear fizzy crowns.

A charmed pineapple tells the joke,
While cantaloupe just starts to choke.
Fruits burst with laughter, such delight,
In this land of sheer insight.

Cherries throw their happy pies,
While ginger roots don silly ties.
All around, the laughter spreads,
With every bite, the humor's fed.

Join the bounty, seize the day,
In fruity fun, we laugh and play.
So come along, don’t miss the thrill,
In brightness, where joy’s the skill.

A Taste of Summer's Veil

In the garden, yellow rays,
A plump fruit strays, oh what a gaze!
Hiding under leaves so green,
What's this riddle, so unseen?

A gentle breeze, a dancing bee,
Is that fruit laughing at me?
Round and bright, it wears a grin,
Come, dear friend, let the fun begin!

Fingers reach for juicy delight,
But wait, it rolls, oh, what a sight!
Chasing shadows round and round,
In this game, no winner found!

At last we sit, tired yet bold,
With stories of this tale retold.
A summer treat, mysterious cheer,
Was it real, or just a smear?

Sweetness in Shadows

Beneath the tree, what do I spy?
A slip of gold, oh me, oh my!
It shimmies left, and dances right,
Is this a fruit or a prank in sight?

With laughter loud and giggles wide,
I tried to catch it, but it sighed!
It rolled away with such a flair,
It seems this fruit just doesn't care!

My friends join in, a merry race,
We chase it down, it's quite the chase!
But just like magic, it takes flight,
Or was it just the breeze at night?

We sit and munch on what we found,
A smaller piece that rolled around.
With sticky fingers, smiles abound,
In shadows sweet, pure joy is bound!

The Elusive Golden Orb

In a sunny patch, a gleam appears,
A golden orb, igniting cheers!
But wait, it wobbles, then rolls away,
Is this a fruit or just a play?

With every step, it takes a leap,
This sneaky orb, it’s hard to keep!
My lunch is near, what can I say?
A fruity chase, let’s start the play!

We trip on roots, we slip on grass,
This merry fruit will never pass!
It hugs a branch, as if it's shy,
A giggling orb, oh me, oh my!

The sun dips low, day turns to night,
In this silly game, it took flight.
But in our hearts, we keep the spark,
Of chasing fruit from dawn till dark!

Secrets of the Succulent Grove

In the grove, where shadows loom,
A secret fruit begins to bloom.
With vibrant skin, it hides in style,
A cheeky smile, oh, what a while!

I tiptoe soft, but it rolls away,
It knows the tricks of silly play.
A bunch of friends now join the fray,
Together we laugh, in fun dismay!

With every tumble, we share a grin,
Is this a game, or just a win?
A fruit so sly, it knows its game,
Oh, who to blame for all this fame?

We sit beneath the leafy shade,
With sticky hands, our smiles displayed.
In every bite, a giggling taste,
The grove will hold our joy, no haste!

In Search of Sunlit Sweetness

In a garden bright and sunny,
A fruit hangs, oh so funny.
Is it ripe, or green with glee?
Let's taste it, and we'll see!

Swings and slides beneath the trees,
Chasing dreams with buzzing bees.
Juicy laughter fills the air,
Who knew fruit could cause such flair?

Sipping nectar, sticky hands,
Making fruit salad plans.
Underneath a swinging vine,
Sweetness is the best design!

With each bite, a smile grows,
Who needs spoons when laughter flows?
In our hunt for sunny cheer,
We’ve found the joy we hold so dear!

Whispers of the Orchard

In the orchard, giggles sprout,
With every twist and every shout.
A riddle here, a chuckle there,
What's that fruit? Who knows, who's aware?

We peek behind the leaves so lush,
Searching for a golden crush.
Is it silly? Is it sad?
Or just the best fruit we ever had?

Bouncing round, trees sway with glee,
Making friends with the buzzing bee.
The air is filled with fruity scents,
What's this treasure? What contents?

In this game of hide and seek,
A juicy prize is what we seek.
So let us laugh, let us cheer,
For the sweetest prize is always near!

Hidden Treasures Beneath the Skin

Underneath a sunny glow,
A treasure waits for us to show.
Peeling back its tough disguise,
A burst of laughter, oh surprise!

With every slice, the mystery thick,
A flavor riddle, oh so quick!
We giggle at the seeds inside,
Like tiny secrets we can't hide.

Juice dribbles down each chin,
Sticky hands are where we begin.
What's this taste? A giggling feat,
Is it sweet, or an epic cheat?

Banana peel's jealous glare,
Orange wonders how it compares.
But nothing beats this fruity fun,
Bright delight beneath the sun!

Tropical Riddles

In a tropical paradise, we dwell,
Fruit that whispers stories to tell.
What’s this puzzle, soft and round?
With every bite, new laughs are found!

They say it’s yellow, but looks quite green,
It’s the quirkiest fruit we’ve ever seen!
Is it a joke, or a fruity prank?
In our tummies, the laughter clanks!

Rolling, bouncing, giggling spree,
Every fruit’s a mystery!
Behind their peeling lies a jest,
Who'll find the silliest, the best?

So together, let’s explore this land,
With ripe surprises in our hand.
Laughter ripens with every taste,
In this fruity race, there’s no haste!

Dreams of the Tropical Breeze

In a garden lush and green,
Tiny fruit hides, seldom seen.
Bright yellow globes on the tree,
Winking at you and me.

Swaying gently, they giggle loud,
Joking with the summer crowd.
A bite so sweet, a flavor burst,
Make your taste buds dance and thirst.

Underneath the sunlit skies,
These golden bulbs tell no lies.
They promise joy with every munch,
Who knew fruit could be so punch?

So chase those whispers, take a leap,
In dreams of fruits, the laughter's deep.
With joy we'll feast, and sing out free,
Oh, what a world of fun! Yippee!

Orchard's Secret Affair

In the orchard, a secret game,
Fruit and laughter are the same.
Sneaky squirrels plan a heist,
Taking fruit is their only vice!

The branches sway with giggles tight,
As critters scurry out of sight.
The fruit invites a merry crew,
Who knew green could turn to blue?

Every day, the sun's decree,
Promises sweetness for you and me.
A fruity dance, a vibrant cheer,
Who knew juice could bring such beer?

With every bite, there's laughter loud,
In this orchard, we're all so proud.
Secrets shared with every taste,
Oh, how we love this fruity haste!

A Journey through Tropical Delights

Let’s embark on a fruity quest,
Tropical lands, they are the best.
Golden fruits with tales galore,
Traveling them could never bore.

With each bite, a giggle shared,
Unforgettable, no one’s scared.
In this wild and zesty array,
Can we eat the brown ones? Nay!

Tasting joy beneath the sun,
A frolic, what a wildly fun run!
Banana peels? Watch your feet!
Oops! The ground's a slippery treat!

From tangy zings to mellow cheer,
These fruits bring laughter, that is clear.
Jump aboard this fruity ride,
Come, let’s share and not divide!

The Golden Enigma Unleashed

In a world of yellow hues,
An enigma awakes, it pursues.
Cheeky smiles, bright as the sun,
What’s this golden treasure? Fun!

With every crunch, the giggles flow,
Golden secrets we now know.
Inside that skin, oh what a taste!
No second guesses, no time to waste!

A puzzling fruit, with charm so rife,
Bringing happiness into life.
Slice it open, what’s inside?
A party for your tongue, take pride!

So gather ‘round, both young and old,
Embrace the wonder, be bold!
In this fruity riddle, laughter echoes,
Let’s eat and dance—come join us, fellows!

Curiosities of the Orchard

In the orchard, fruits reside,
With hidden secrets they confide.
One tree sways with a wink and grin,
It tempts my taste buds to begin.

A creature grumbles from its nest,
Claiming mangoes, that's the best!
But wait, does it share its score?
Or gobbles them all, who could ignore?

With swinging branches way up high,
I wonder how they touch the sky.
Each plump fruit's a joke to taste,
Yet every bite is gone in haste!

A riddle wrapped in skin so bright,
Why are they elusive, out of sight?
I laugh as I chase every clue,
In this orchard's game, I'm a fool too!

Perusing the Tropical Canvas

A canvas painted, bold and bright,
With colors swirling pure delight.
I wander through this fruity maze,
In search of flavors to amaze.

One fruit shouts ‘pick me, I’m the one!’
But another giggles, just for fun.
I grab a handful, drop a few,
It dances around, oh what to do?

A parrot squawks, ‘You’ll never stay!’
As I juggle them in a playful display.
Each bite bursts like a comedy show,
Laughter fills the air, oh what a flow!

The tropical breeze brings secrets untold,
Of flavor battles, both brave and bold.
Each drippy slice brings giggles to share,
In this amusing fruit-filled affair!

Sunlit Whispers of Delight

Under the sun, giggles spring,
As fruity wonders dance and sing.
A bright yellow burst of cheer,
Bringing smiles from ear to ear.

The wind whispers, ‘Give it a try,
For in this fruit, you’ll touch the sky!’
I bite and squeal in big surprise,
Delights unfold before my eyes.

A sipping contest with juice so true,
The sticky dribbles, a silly brew.
Tropical treasures, what a sight!
Every flavor takes flight in the light.

I sing with joy, ‘Oh, what a treat!’
In this orchard, no one can beat.
A laughter riot, sunshine held,
In this sweet adventure, all is compelled!

The Golden Dilemma

In the golden light, a fruit parade,
Teasing my senses, a tasty charade.
I ponder which one is ripe to munch,
As squirrels giggle, 'Join the crunch!'

They scuffle and tumble, what a sight,
With silly antics that bring pure delight.
I reach for one and it rolls away,
Such playful trickery, oh what a day!

A fruit with sparkles, a riot of fun,
'Pick me,' it shouts, 'I'm number one!'
But just then a bird swoops low,
With a cheeky laugh, it steals the show.

I'm left with crumbs as they flap and fly,
Yet joy fills my heart, and I cannot lie.
For every moment holds laughter's claim,
In this golden whimsy, all is the same!

Exploring the Hues of Curiosity

In the garden, bright and bold,
Laughter echoes, tales unfold.
A splash of yellow, a twist of green,
What on earth could this fruit mean?

A curious creature peeks with glee,
Is it a snack, or just a tree?
With every bite, a joke takes flight,
Oh, the flavors dance in delight!

Who knew a fruit could wear a grin?
Is it the sweetness, or simply skin?
A giggle escapes with each juicy taste,
In this fruity charade, there's no time to waste!

So gather your friends, let the fun ignite,
In this playful world, everything's bright.
With every munch, a chuckle shared,
In this fruity adventure, no one is scared!

The Fruit’s Delicate Secret

Beneath the skin, a tale so sweet,
With hidden flavors that skip a beat.
A wink from the fruit, a playful tease,
It’s a treasure hunt, if you please!

One bite in, and laughter rings,
Juice-covered faces, oh the silly things!
It's not just fruit; it's a party here,
Whirling and twirling, spreading cheer!

What sorcery lies in this golden sphere?
A fruit that giggles, oh how queer!
Did it just chuckle, or was it me?
This delicious charade brings glee, oh glee!

Come one, come all, let’s crack the code,
In this fruity mystery, we'll burst, explode!
With joy in our hearts and stains on our face,
Let's savor the laughter, this fruity embrace!

Temple of the Tropical Muse

Welcome, dear friend, to the temple's delight,
Where colors collide, and the flavors ignite.
A fruit on the altar, so round and so bright,
Whispers of joy, in the soft, fading light.

It's a place of worship, for taste buds divine,
Where giggles are currency, laughter the wine.
We worship the sweetness, and one another,
In this temple of tropics, where we're all like brothers!

With every slice, a spell is cast,
A joyful riddle, what a blast!
A toss of the fruit, it rides the breeze,
Sending giggles and joy across the trees

So raise your feast, let merriment flow,
In this fruity sanctuary, join the show!
With smiles so broad and hearts so light,
In the temple of joy, everything feels right!

Honeyed Hues of Mystery

In the honeyed glow, a secret hides,
With every bite, the laughter slides.
A burst of sweetness, oh so fine,
Is this a treat, or just a sign?

Wrapped in colors, a playful disguise,
It’s not just fruit, but joyous surprise!
Each juicy morsel, a giggle in tow,
What will we find? We never know!

As comrades gather, the tasting begins,
Silly faces and fruity spins.
A slice shared, and oh what a thrill,
In the realm of flavors, we find our fill!

So come one, come all, let’s munch and share,
In this honeyed realm, there's love everywhere!
With every chuckle and each silly cheer,
In the dance of delight, there’s nothing to fear!

The Taste of Hidden Desires

In the garden ripe and bright,
A fruit that sparks delight.
It juggles sweetness in its skin,
A giggle waits where tastes begin.

With flavors secret, oh so bold,
It leaves us craving, uncontrolled.
Each bite a tease, a playful jest,
Will it be sour, or just the best?

The juice drips down in summer's heat,
A puzzle wrapped in sunny sweet.
We chase the thrill, a chasing game,
In hopes to taste the fruit of fame.

But when I reach, it slips away,
My friends all laugh, and cutelay.
That fruit just grins, it can’t be caught,
In playful jest, it leaves me fraught.

A Dip in Citrus Mystique

A splash of zest upon my tongue,
A riddle sung, a song unslung.
In citrus tang, I take my dive,
To find the truth where flavors thrive.

With every sip, a giggle slips,
A waltz of tastes on glossy lips.
I ponder hard, what's this allure?
A citrus fortune, ripe and pure?

The trees all chuckle in the sun,
As I explore this fruiting fun.
I stumble here, I flip and roll,
While citrus scents entwine my soul.

Am I a fruit detective now?
With silly hats, I take a bow.
The quest for zest fills me with glee,
In citrus dreams, I'll never flee.

Lush Landscapes and Leafy Secrets

In shadows green, the whispers play,
Among the leaves, a game today.
The hidden bits, with secrets rife,
In every corner, sparks of life.

I wander wide, with curious eyes,
To find the truth where laughter lies.
A bud of joy upon each branch,
In leafy realms, we take our chance.

Each step I take brings smiles anew,
A giggling breeze, a merry view.
I poke and prod, then dance around,
As nature's jokes are all around.

But then a tug, my shoe's stuck tight,
I tug and laugh, oh what a sight!
In leafy charm, I lose my way,
A funny twist at end of day.

The Scent of Paradise

In fragrant blooms, imagination soars,
I chase the scents behind closed doors.
With noses high, we sniff and roam,
In fruity dreams, we find our home.

The aromatic tales unwind,
With scents of bliss, they tease the mind.
Each whiff a prank, a cheeky joke,
That tickles silly, like a poke.

In laughter's air, the blossoms sing,
A funny riddle spring to spring.
Around the corner, scents collide,
In this paradise, I take a ride.

But oh, what’s this? A noseful snare,
I tumble down – the scent’s a flare!
And here I lie, with giggles loud,
In sweetened dreams, I feel quite proud.

Secrets Buried in Green Shadows

In the garden blooms a riddle,
With whispers hiding in the leaves,
A fruit so round, a cheeky giggle,
It plays pretend and never grieves.

Beneath the shade, the stories frolic,
As squirrels dance and birds critique,
A plotting crew, both sly and comic,
What’s ripe today? Oh, so mystique!

Each bite’s a chance, a gamble sweet,
With sticky hands and laughter loud,
The juice drips down, a fruity treat,
And secrets hide in playful crowd.

So gather ‘round, let’s crack the code,
In shadows thick, we’ll have some fun,
For every laugh, there’s sweeter road,
The game of fruits has just begun.

Echoes of a Swaying Branch

A branch above sways like a jester,
With hidden prizes, what a jest!
The fruit just teases, quite the tester,
It’s shouting, ‘Come, you’ll love the quest!’

Underneath, we plot and leap,
To catch the prizes hanging high,
But slippery tales make laughter seep,
As we stumble, oh me, oh my!

With every bounce, our joy is swelling,
The branch responds with playful sprout,
A merry dance, the fruit is yelling,
‘You're chasing dreams, oh, what a route!’

So off we go, in giggles’ trance,
To swing and sway in laughter’s air,
With echoes bold, we join the dance,
And leave behind our worries bare.

The Allure of Dappled Sunshine

In sunlight patches, treasures glow,
A splash of gold, like giggles bright,
We chase the shimmer, to and fro,
Each bite's a punchline to delight.

A dance of shadows, light's ballet,
With fruit enticing from the trees,
It winks and nods, come out to play,
To share some joy, a laugh, a breeze.

With sticky fingers, cheers resound,
A jubilee of fruity fun,
Each scrumptious bite, a king unbound,
Each giggle shared, we all have won.

So let's embrace this sunny prank,
With every taste, the world feels fine,
In dappled light, we give our thanks,
For laughter comes on every vine.

Chasing the Velvet Aroma

A scent so rich, it leads us near,
With noses twitching, hearts in flight,
The velvet aroma, sweet and clear,
It's calling out, 'Come, take a bite!'

In every corner, giggles sprout,
As we embark on this grand chase,
The fruit's a tease, a playful doubt,
Our laughter's bright, a joyous race.

Beneath the tree, we plan our heist,
With whispers hushed, we sneak and peer,
To snatch the prize of fruity spice,
A banquet laid, with grins sincere.

So here we are, in fruity bliss,
Chasing scents that make us sing,
With every bloom, there's love and kiss,
In this wild tale, we're everything!

Fruits of Clandestine Whispers

In the market, fruits conspire,
Bananas giggle, they never tire.
A pear sneezes, oh what a fright!
Grapes tumble down, a cheeky sight.

But one stands out, all shiny and bright,
With whispers of secrets, a daring bite.
Could it be sweet, or a trick up its peel?
Laughter erupts, it's a fruit that's surreal!

Oranges spin tales of zest and cheer,
While cherries know gossip we love to hear.
A rambutan's hair is a curious shock,
Its fuzzy demeanor can shift like a clock.

So gather your fruits, let the fun commence,
In the land of flavors, it all feels intense.
Each bite a riddle, each taste a jest,
In this fruity world, we're surely blessed!

A Journey through Golden Echoes

Off we go on a fruity ride,
With bananas that giggle, side by side.
A pineapple wears a dapper crown,
As coconuts shout, ‘Don’t be a clown!’

Grapes throw confetti, oh what a scene,
Their tiny voices call out, ‘Let’s be seen!’
Lemonade smiles, but don't squeeze too hard,
For sour surprises may leave you charred!

The mango struts, in a hue so bright,
It winks at the crowd, what a silly sight!
“Am I sweet or tart? Come take a taste!”
With laughs and giggles, we’ll not go to waste.

In this journey of flavors, we dance and twirl,
With fruity friends, let imaginations swirl.
Each bite a chuckle, a flavor so bold,
In this land of echoes, our stories unfold.

Sweet Illusions in the Grove

Deep in the grove, where the wild fruits play,
The berries throw parties, hip hip hooray!
With peaches in hats and kiwi that sings,
They swirl in circles, oh, what joy it brings!

A fig tells a joke about being so sweet,
But don't let it fool you; it can’t take the heat.
Cantaloupes chuckle as they roll on the ground,
With laughter contagious, it's pure joy abound.

A lychee giggles, its textured delight,
Its friends all rally, ‘This fruit’s outta sight!’
Pineapple sings songs of adventure and fun,
While each little berry jives under the sun.

In this grove of illusions, we dance through the day,
With flavor and laughter, nothing fades away.
So join all the fruits, let the merriment start,
For life’s a sweet riddle and we’re playing our part!

Whirling Tastes of the Tropics

Dance to the rhythm of tropical cheer,
With fruits that frolic, no worries or fear.
A rambutan giggles, its hair flying high,
While sassy durians plot in the sky.

Bananas divide into paths of delight,
Their pranks bring mischief to day and to night.
A mango sneezes, and juice goes everywhere,
It winks at the crowd, oh what a flair!

In this whirlwind of flavors, we swirl and we spin,
With grapefruits trying their best for a win.
A juicy contest, who's the funniest fruit?
As we munch and we laugh, there's no need to compute.

So raise up your hands, let the laughter erupt,
Tropical fruits know just how to disrupt.
With sweet bursts of fun and those wild, silly moves,
In this whirling dance, everybody grooves!

Tropical Secrets Unveiled

In the grove, a laugh we hear,
Fruits are dancing, never fear.
A pink elephant strolls by,
Wearing shades beneath the sky.

They speak of sweetness in disguise,
With giggles, they spin and rise.
One fruit claims it knows the tale,
Of a snail that dared to sail.

A parrot squawks, 'It's all a game!'
'Who knew fruits could take such fame?'
A monkey swings and pretends to write,
Stories of a fruit that’s quite a sight!

With every bite, a new surprise,
Juicy tales from fruity guys.
So grab your fork, take a peek,
For more secrets, come and seek!

Juicy Whispers of the Orchard

In the orchard, whispers play,
Fruits gossip through the day.
One says it dreams of being pie,
While another just wants to fly.

A fig in plaid, a pear in stripes,
Join the dance of fruity types.
They tell of plans to rule the land,
With a fruity crown so grand!

The watermelon wears a hat,
He dances, looking quite the brat.
So much fun in every bite,
Who knew fruits were such a sight?

They share their dreams, their wild hopes,
Creating juice from juicy tropes.
With laughter ripe and spirits high,
In the orchard, oh how they'll fly!

Beneath the Golden Skin

Beneath the golden skin so bright,
Lies a party, oh what a sight!
A fruit in sneakers, doing a jig,
While another one rocks a pink wig.

They share their secrets, tales of flair,
A squishy debate, who’s the fairest there?
Coconuts drop, they cheer with glee,
'Hey, join the show, it’s free!' they plea.

With a wink and a juicy squeeze,
Lemons burst forth with cheeky ease.
'The juiciest squeeze is yet to come!'
As limes roll and drum the rhyme of fun!

So peel away and take a taste,
The laughter, never goes to waste.
For beneath the skin, the stories spin,
In this fruity world, let the fun begin!

Enigma of the Sun-Kissed Fruit

In the sun, a riddle blooms,
Amongst the trees, the laughter zooms.
A cheeky lime with a sassy grin,
Claims it knows where the fun begins.

With hints of bubblegum and spice,
These fruits insist, 'We’re oh so nice!'
A watermelon tries to tell a joke,
But ends up making everyone choke.

They frolic and spin, a fruity dance,
With mangoes clad in polka dots, they prance.
They compete for who can make the best pie,
While pretending that fruits can fly high.

So join the party, don’t be shy,
Let the fruity laughter amplify.
For in this grove, beneath the sun,
The enigma is — all fruits just want fun!

Behind the Fruit's Embrace

In a garden bright, where the laughter swells,
Fruits hide their secrets, only time tells.
A cheeky breeze stirs, teasing dreams awake,
Whispers of sweetness, what mischief they'll make.

The yellow glow calls, with a wink and a grin,
Peeling back layers, let the fun begin!
In the realm of the fruit, so carefree and spry,
Who knew that a bite could make you fly high?

Flavors dance wildly, with each playful toss,
Chasing the taste, never counting the cost.
From the branch to the bowl, they giggle and cheer,
Creating a ruckus, now that summer's here.

So gather around for a fruity delight,
The joy in the air is simply just right.
Behind each bright skin, there's a joke tucked away,
Come join in the fun, let the laughter stay!

The Allure of Ambrosial Shadows

Beneath leafy shades, where the sun beams up,
Fruits whisper softly, 'Come take a sup!'
With laughter they beckon from every small glade,
Unraveling secrets, their charm never fades.

A toss of the fruit, and the giggles ignite,
In the cool of the shade, it feels just right.
Biting into sweetness, the world's spin in bliss,
Who knew serious fruit could be wrapped in such wit?

With flavors that tickle and colors that shine,
The mischief unravels, sip from this vine.
Tales of the orchard, unroll like a scroll,
Every juicy morsel, a story to unroll.

In shadows of laughter, we gather to play,
Chasing the giggles, they’re never far away.
What a puzzling riddle set on the vine,
Opening fruit is like sipping on time!

Unspooling the Fruitful Tale

Nestled in branches, stories abound,
A fruity adventure waiting to be found.
Peeking and poking, with pure delight,
What wonders await on this warm, sunny night?

The scent in the air is a curious tease,
Dancing with doubt, about what comes with ease.
Each nibble reveals what the trees want to say,
With giggles and grins, we relish the play.

Bouncing and rolling, they splat on the ground,
Fruitful escapades that spin round and round.
With a splash and a pop, what a raucous surprise,
Surrounded by laughter, let joy truly rise.

At the center of fun, there lies a soft core,
Fruits never tire, they keep wanting more.
Unspool this adventure, let the flavors unfold,
In bites of bright humor, a tale to be told!

Sweetness in a Whispering Breeze

When zephyrs come calling on a bright sunny day,
Fruits giggle and chuckle, come join in their play.
With each gentle breath, secrets flit on through,
A world full of laughter, waiting just for you.

They twirl through the air with a teasing allure,
In a dance of the wind, the tropics are pure.
Sweetness unfurls like a mischievous sprite,
Crafting tales of joy, hidden well out of sight.

With colors so vivid, they play peek-a-boo,
Every juicy moment, a burst of the new.
Boundless in flavor, like whispers they ease,
Each fruit has a jest wrapped within its sweet breeze.

So gather them up, let the fun now commence,
Join in the laughter, let your taste buds commence.
In a world where the breezes and giggles unite,
Embrace all the sweetness, let merriment ignite!

A Palette of Tropical Dreams

In the orchard, colors burst,
Yellow, green, in merry thrust,
A fruit that winks, a cheeky tease,
Caught in sunlight, swaying trees.

Lemon's cousin, tales unfold,
Sticky fingers, treasures bold,
Dancing on the tongue's delight,
One big bite, oh what a sight!

The juice drips down, a sugary trick,
Watch your shirt, oh snap, too slick!
Giggles echo in the sun,
Chasing bliss, we all have fun.

What’s this fruit, just can’t decide,
Is it nature’s jester, full of pride?
Laughter ripens in every slice,
This tropical dream, oh so nice!

Sour and Sweet: A Duality

Two faces share one skin,
One grins wide, one wears a grin,
Biting in, a sharp surprise,
A tug of war, we compromise.

Sweet as honey, bold and bright,
Then it stings with a zesty bite,
Like a prank pulled by a friend,
Ready, set, let the fun extend!

The laughter echoes, can’t ignore,
A fruit that keeps us wanting more,
A jester dressed in yellow hue,
What's your flavor? The choice is due!

Can’t complain, I’ll take the ride,
This dual game, oh what a glide,
In every slice, a story sings,
Sour and sweet, oh, how it clings!

The Flavorful Paradox

A tasty riddle, oh what fun,
Tangy tales on tongues run,
Juicy secrets burst and tease,
A playful vibe in every breeze.

In the kitchen, chaos reigns,
Sticky fingers, sweet remains,
One bite smiles, the next a shock,
This fruity jester’s quite a knock!

Unpeel the laughter, slice it wide,
What’s wrapped inside, we can’t decide,
A twist awaits with every taste,
The paradox, not to waste!

Oh, swing your fork and take a leap,
With every chew, the laughter peeps,
Frontal giggles in the air,
Each juicy bite’s a lover's dare!

Confessions of a Ripe Heart

What hides inside this juicy shell?
Secrets dance and giggles swell,
In sunlit patches, hearts align,
Ripeness whispers, 'Taste me fine!'

The boldness calls, a daring choice,
Sweet or sour, hear the voice,
Unravel layers, each bite's a clue,
What kind of love awaits for you?

Cheeky smiles beneath the skin,
With every munch, the fun begins,
A riddle wrapped in tropical zest,
Confessions shared, we're truly blessed!

So come and join the flavor spree,
Life's a ride, come share with me,
With laughter echoing, dreams take flight,
In every nibble, pure delight!

Hues of Sunset in a Single Slice

In the orchard, colors gleam,
Golden globes, a juicy dream.
Slices served with laughter wide,
Tastebuds dance, let joy abide.

Beneath the tree, we sneak a bite,
Sweetness drips, a pure delight.
We giggle at the sticky mess,
Nature's gift, we must confess.

Peeling skins and giggling loud,
Underneath the thick green shroud.
Who knew such joy would come to be,
In a fruit as bright as we can see?

So join us in this silly feast,
From sunset hues, we’ll never cease.
With a slice in hand, we'll run and play,
In this fruity fun, we'll surely stay.

Secrets of the Orchard's Heart

Beneath the leaves, a treasure hides,
Laughter echoes; it abides.
Fruits that giggle, tease, and twirl,
Each one a jester in a swirl.

Climbing high for that sweet bite,
Falling down, oh what a sight!
The orchard’s laughter fills the air,
Secrets woven everywhere.

With juice that splatters on our face,
We race around in silly chase.
Under the sun, we leap and bound,
In these moments, joy is found.

So take a dip in nature's smile,
Savor the fun, stay for a while.
With every laugh, the truth’s in sight,
That simple joys make life so bright.

The Ripe Allure of Nature's Gift

Oh, the allure of golden skin,
With every bite, we grin and spin.
A treasure trove of laughter waits,
In every fruit, mischief creates.

Slicing through, the juice will fly,
In every drop, we wonder why.
Like a painter, colors clash,
A juicy canvas, what a splash!

With giggles rising to the tree,
Nature’s art, wild and free.
The fruit of glee, oh what a sight,
In this dance, we feel so light.

So come, my friends; let’s join the cheer,
With ripe delights, we’ll shed our fear.
In this orchard, let’s take a stand,
For nature's gift, so sweet and grand.

Flickers of Taste and Time

In the garden where laughter grows,
Slicing fruit, we strike a pose.
Every flavor sparks delight,
Underneath the sun so bright.

Time stands still as juices flow,
With every bite, our joy will show.
We share the smiles, hugs, and laughs,
In this fruit-filled world, our hearts are vast.

Achievements come from sticky hands,
As we explore nature’s funny plans.
Chasing flavors through the day,
In playful cheer, the worries sway.

So dance beneath the fruity skies,
With every squirt, we feel so wise.
In every moment, we take delight,
With flickers of taste, everything’s right.

Riddles of the Ripening Tree

Underneath the leafy shade,
A fruit hangs, daring to evade.
It's sweet, it's green, it’s never shy,
But who knows why it waves goodbye?

A squirrel spies with curious eyes,
He schemed and plotted, oh, what a spy!
With tiny paws full of delight,
He questions if it’s day or night.

A giggle ripples through the breeze,
“Is it ready? Oh, please, oh please!”
The branches shake with ripe suspense,
As laughter echoes, so immense!

So next time you see a glowing orb,
Remember the tree that loves to absorb.
A riddle wrapped in golden hue,
Will keep the giggles fresh and new.

Nectar of the Exotic Realm

In a land where sweetness reigns,
A fruity joke on sunshine's plains.
With flavors bold and laughter bright,
Who’ll take a taste and savor right?

The parrot squawks with envy loud,
For juicy dreams are born from crowd.
With every bite, it’s giggle galore,
As juice dribbles from mouth to floor.

Two ants debate, with tiny hands,
On which one’s best from sun-kissed lands.
One claims green, the other gold,
Around the world, their tale is told.

Oh, nectar flows from tree to lace,
In fruity games, we find our place.
A slice of joy, a splash of cheer,
The exotic smiles draw us near.

The Color of Summer Dreams

Bright hues dance in summer's light,
As citrus laughs and takes to flight.
Oh, swirls of yellow, hints of green,
A colorful puzzle yet unseen!

So what's the hue? They all debate,
The fruit's a joker, oh how great!
With peels of sunshine, creamy bliss,
A fruity riddle sealed with a kiss.

Kids on bikes race past the grove,
They giggle softly, as if in love.
One bites in joy, without a care,
And shouts, "Let's paint the world, I swear!"

In this carnival of fruity cheer,
With every taste, we bring it near.
A palette ripe with stories spun,
Summer smiles for everyone!

Ancient Tales of the Juicy Flesh

Once upon a time, oh so sweet,
Lived a fruit with tricks and beats.
Legends whisper in every peel,
“Can you handle what we conceal?”

The wise old owl perched high on bough,
Cackles with tales, you know not how.
“My dear friends, it’s quite absurd,
This juicy riddle’s never heard!”

With playful schemes from dusk till dawn,
The juicy orb continues on.
How many bites does it take to share?
With laughs and cheers, we fill the air!

So gather ‘round, let stories flow,
Of ancient tales that make us glow.
For every fruit holds laughter’s key,
Unlock the joy—a mystery!

www.ingramcontent.com/pod-product-compliance
Lightning Source LLC
Chambersburg PA
CBHW060134230426
43661CB00003B/414
* 9 7 8 1 8 0 5 8 6 3 5 5 7 *